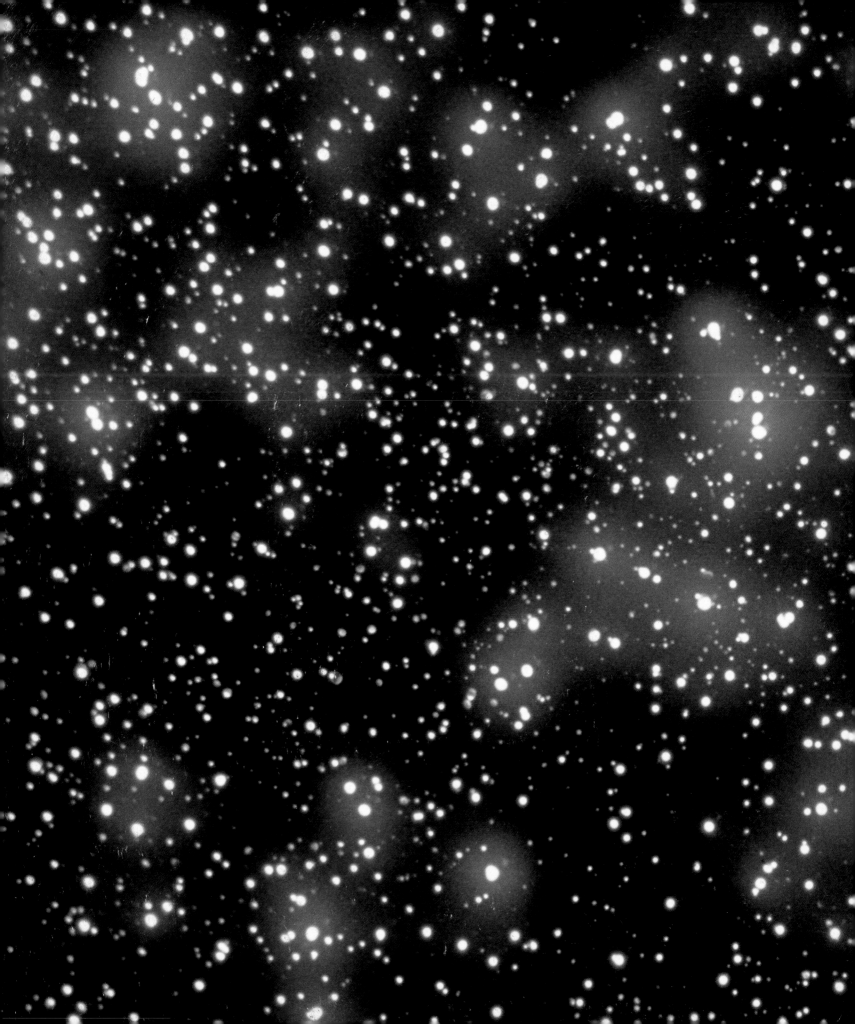

# GALAXIES

## Michael George

CREATIVE EDUCATION

Designed by Rita Marshall
with the help of Thomas Lawton

© 1992 Creative Education, Inc.
123 South Broad Street,
Mankato, Minnesota 56001

Photography by Peter Arnold, FPG
International, Image Bank, Photri,
Photo Network, Photo Researchers,
Frank Rossotto, and Visuals
Unlimited

Library of Congress
Cataloging-in-Publication Data

George, Michael, 1964–
Galaxies / by Michael George.
    p.   cm.
Describes our Milky Way and
considers the scientific probability
that our universe contains about 100
billion additional galaxies, each with
an average of 100 billion stars.
ISBN 0-88682-433-8.
1. Galaxies—Juvenile literature.
[1. Galaxies.]  I. Title.  91-8223
QB857.3.G46   1991        CIP
523.1'12—dc20              AC

*Each night, thousands of stars decorate* the deep, dark sky. On dark, moonless nights, we can also see a faint band of light stretching across the sky. This hazy cloud of light is produced by millions of distant stars. The stars are so far away that they cannot be distinguished as separate specks of light. All of these stars, from the brightest to the dimmest, belong to an enormous group of stars called a *Galaxy*.

*The Milky Way.*

If we could see this entire cluster of stars, known as the Milky Way galaxy, it would look like an enormous, flattened disk of stars. The galaxy has three long spiral arms that wrap around a bulge in the center. The spiral arms contain many millions of stars, but most of the stars are packed together in the *Central Bulge*. In all, scientists estimate that the Milky Way galaxy contains 200 billion stars. If you counted one star every second, it would take six thousand years to count all the stars in the Milky Way.

*A galaxy's central bulge.*
*Inset: The spiral arms of the Milky Way.*

One of the stars in the Milky Way galaxy is our own star, the Sun. The *Solar System,* which includes the Sun, the Earth, and the other eight planets, is not located in the center of the galaxy. Instead, it lies about two-thirds of the way out in one of the spiral arms. Because of our location in the Milky Way, we have two different views of our galaxy from Earth. When we look away from the plane of our galaxy, we see few stars. But when we look at our galaxy edge on, we see so many distant stars that they blend together to form a hazy cloud of light across the sky.

*The brightest part of our galaxy.*

The stars that make up the Milky Way galaxy continuously spin around the central bulge. The Sun and our Solar System speed around the center of the galaxy at over six hundred thousand miles per hour. We do not notice this motion because everything around us is moving at the same pace. Even traveling at this tremendous speed, it takes our Solar System more than 200 million years to circle around the center of the galaxy.

Our galaxy is so enormous that its size is difficult to comprehend. Today's spaceships are far too slow to explore the Milky Way. It would take our fastest rocket thousands of years just to reach the star nearest to our Sun. In order to explore our galaxy, we would need to travel near *The Speed of Light*, the fastest speed possible in the universe. Light travels 187,000 miles every second, or nearly 700 million miles per hour.

*A timed exposure of the night sky.*

14

Although scientists have not yet discovered a way to travel at the speed of light, imagine that we can hop on the next light beam leaving the Earth and venture to the center of the Milky Way. Moments after leaving the Earth, we flash by the Moon. Seconds later we streak by Mars. Within five minutes, we pass Jupiter, Saturn, Uranus, and Neptune. Only ten minutes after leaving the Earth, we speed by Pluto and leave our Solar System far behind. Already, the Sun looks no different from the other stars in the sky.

After leaving our Solar System, the scenery becomes rather monotonous. The sights become less spectacular and far less frequent. Weeks pass, and we see nothing but familiar stars dotting the black sky. Months creep by, but there are still no new stars or planets. Even in the cloud of stars we call the Milky Way, the universe is mostly empty space.

*The stars are trillions of miles apart.*
*Inset: Halley's comet streaks through space.*

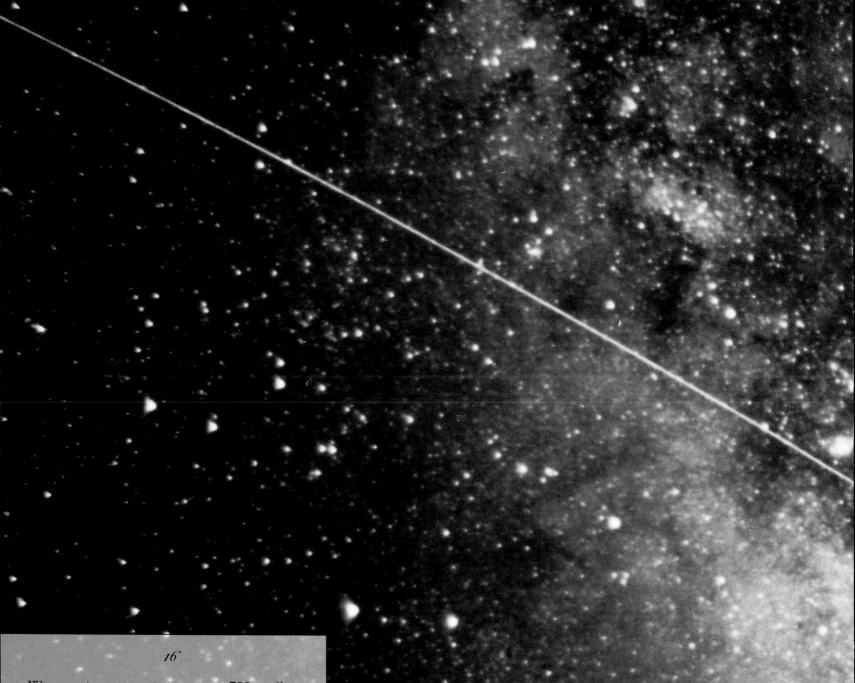

We continue our journey at 700 million miles per hour toward the center of our galaxy. Eventually, an entire year passes. Racing through our galaxy at the speed of light for 365 straight days, we have traveled nearly six trillion miles. Scientists call this distance, the distance that light travels in a year, a *Light-year*. A light-year is a measure of distance, just like a mile, but it is a far greater distance.

After traveling for one year at the speed of light, we have traveled one light-year from Earth. Our journey continues. Years pass, and still we see nothing new. Finally, after traveling for about four years, we streak past our first star. As quickly as the star comes into view, it disappears behind us. The monotony continues. Although we travel as fast as possible, we make little progress toward the center of the Milky Way.

*Light travels through space at nearly 700 million miles per hour.*

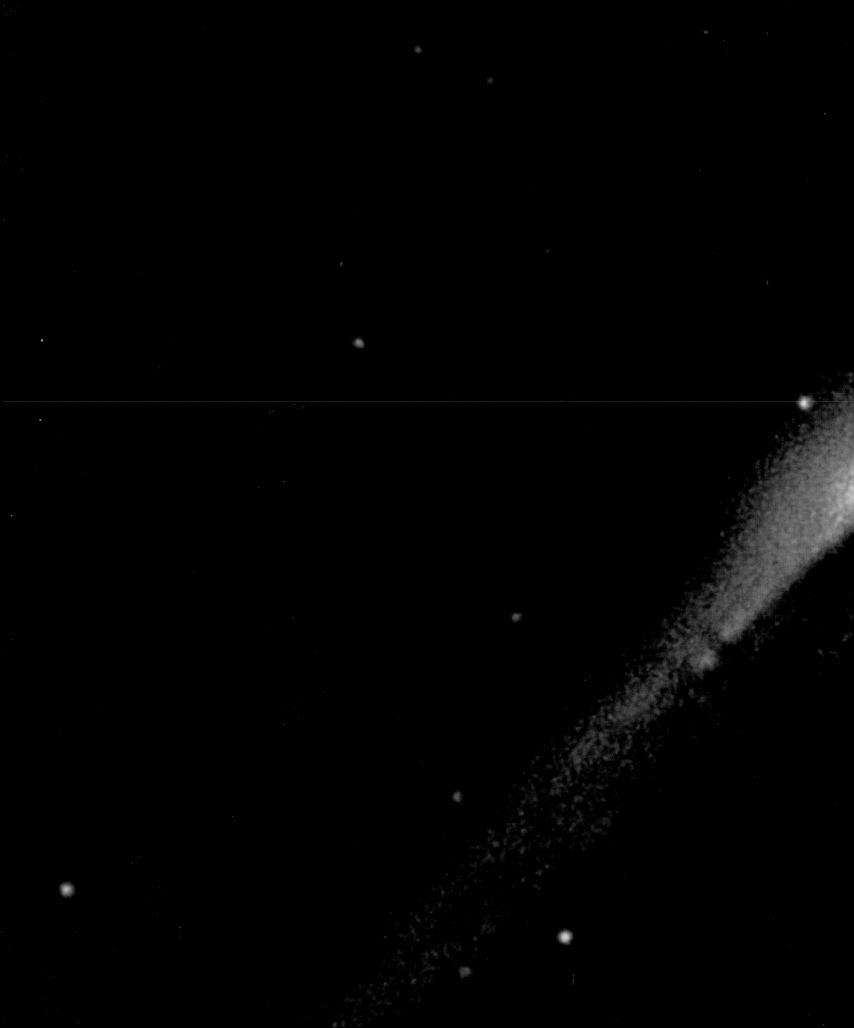

Every few years we pass another star, or perhaps a giant cloud of gas and dust. During our lifetimes, the scenery changes little. If we could travel for a hundred years, or even a thousand years, we would still be far from the center of the galaxy. In order to reach the center of the Milky Way we would need to travel at the speed of light for about thirty thousand years. Obviously, the Milky Way galaxy is an enormous region of space.

As gigantic as the Milky Way seems, it is not the only galaxy in the universe. Peering past the stars in our own galaxy with powerful telescopes, scientists can see other galaxies sprinkled throughout space. Scientists group the galaxies according to their shapes. They have identified three basic types of galaxies: spiral, elliptical, and irregular.

*Galaxies are classified according to their shapes.*

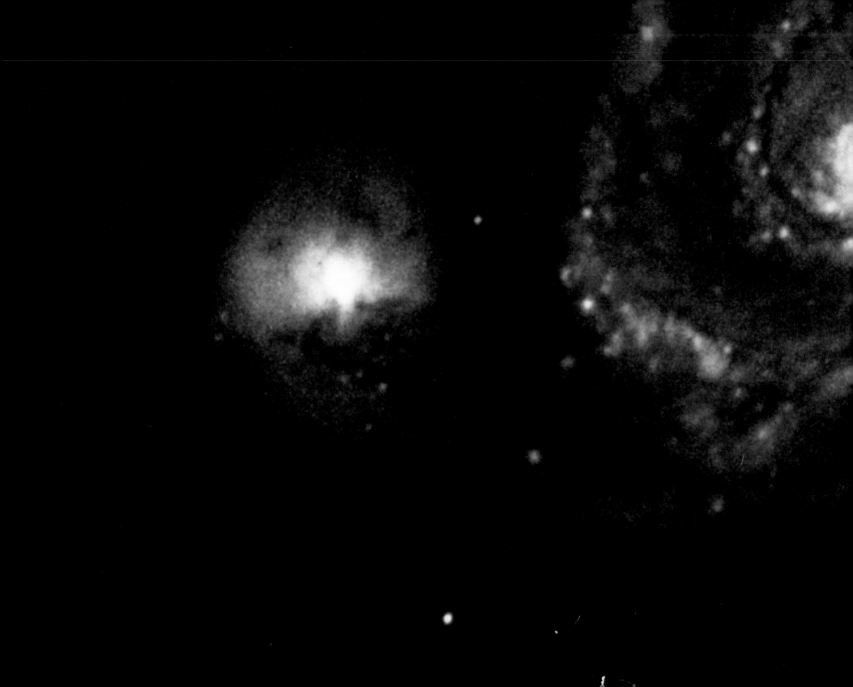

*Spiral galaxies* are similar to the Milky Way, with long, spiral arms that wrap around a central bulge. The spiral pattern differs from one galaxy to the next. The spiral arms can be very tightly wound, or they may be more open. The central bulge can be huge in relation to the arms, or it may be very small and compact. Some spiral galaxies, called *Barred Spirals*, have bands of stars and dust running through their centers.

*A spiral galaxy.*

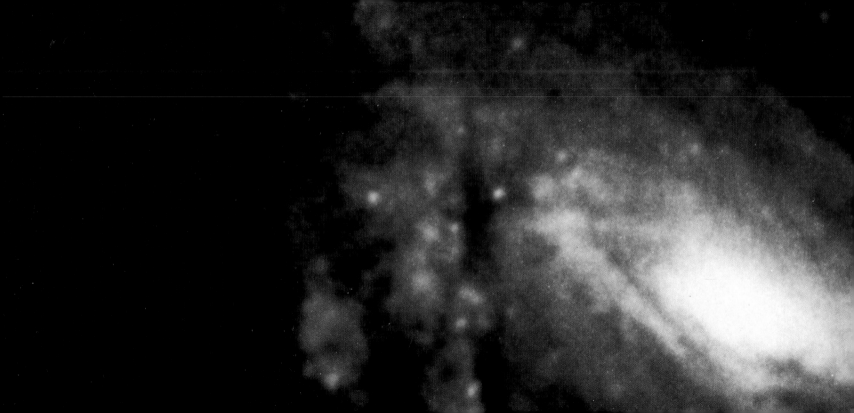

The *Elliptical Galaxy* is the most common type of galaxy in the universe. Elliptical galaxies are round or oval in shape. They look like spiral galaxies without spiraling arms. A few elliptical galaxies are many times larger than the Milky Way; however, most elliptical galaxies, called *Dwarf Ellipticals,* are very small compared to spiral galaxies. While our own galaxy is one hundred thousand light-years across, some dwarf galaxies are only a few thousand light-years wide.

---

*Spiral galaxies are usually much larger than elliptical galaxies.*

Unlike spiral and elliptical galaxies, *Irregular Galaxies* do not have any definite shape. Irregular galaxies may appear as rings, stretched-out groups of stars, or a variety of other shapes. Scientists believe that irregular galaxies form when two galaxies collide or brush past each other. Amazingly, when galaxies pass through other galaxies there are few, if any, stellar collisions. The vast distances between stars prevent this. However, the gravity of each galaxy pulls on the other and distorts its shape.

*Irregular galaxies.*

Galaxies are not spread uniformly throughout the universe. Instead, they tend to swarm together in clusters. The Milky Way belongs to a cluster of galaxies called the *Local Group*. Scientists estimate that there are thirty galaxies in the Local Group. They are unsure of the exact number because dust and debris in the Milky Way may hide the faintest galaxies. The largest galaxy in the Local Group is the *Andromeda galaxy,* containing over 300 billion stars.

*Andromeda galaxy.*

With about thirty galaxies, each containing billions of stars, the Local Group is an enormous collection of stars. However, it is a small cluster of galaxies when compared with other clusters in the universe. The *Coma Cluster*, for instance, may contain over ten thousand galaxies. In all, scientists estimate that our universe contains about 100 billion galaxies, each with an average of 100 billion stars.

From one edge to the other, the Milky Way galaxy spans about one hundred thousand light-years. While this is an enormous distance, even greater distances separate the Milky Way from other galaxies. The Andromeda galaxy, for example, is two million light-years from the Milky Way. The distance to other clusters of galaxies is even more remarkable. Scientists estimate that the Coma Cluster lies an astonishing 100 million light-years from the Local Group.

*A cluster of galaxies in the Coma Berenices constellation.*

When considering distant galaxies, it is important to keep something in mind. Imagine that you are on a star, five light-years from Earth, and your parents give you a new bike for your birthday. You want to show it to your best friend who is back on Earth. Since you know that light travels faster than anything, you send a picture of your new bike back to Earth on the next light beam leaving the star. How long does it take for the beam of light, and the picture of your bike, to reach the Earth?

*Centaurus galaxy.*

### 33

Although light travels faster than anything in our universe, it does not travel instantaneously. In fact, as you know, light travels exactly one light-year in one year. Therefore, light travels five light-years, the distance back to Earth, in five years. In other words, it takes five years for the beam of light, and the picture of your bike, to reach your friend. Although your friend would think your bike was brand new, it would already be five years old. By then, you might even have a new bike.

*Two globular star clusters.*

The light beams we see from distant galaxies are actually images of the galaxies, similar to the picture of your bike. However, rather than being five light-years away like the imaginary star, galaxies are millions of light-years from Earth. The light we see from other galaxies has been traveling through space for millions of years. Therefore, we do not see the distant galaxies as they are right now; we see images of them as they were millions of years ago.

*Clouds of dust in space.*

Beyond even the farthest galaxies, scientists have discovered bizarre objects called *Quasars*. In order to be detected from Earth, quasars must radiate enormous amounts of energy. Scientists estimate that one quasar can radiate as much energy as ten thousand galaxies. This tremendous amount of energy flows from a region slightly larger than our Solar System. How so much energy can be generated in such a small area is a major question in astronomy. No known process, not even a continuous nuclear explosion, can produce the amount of energy released by a quasar.

*Crab nebula, the gaseous remains of a dying star.*

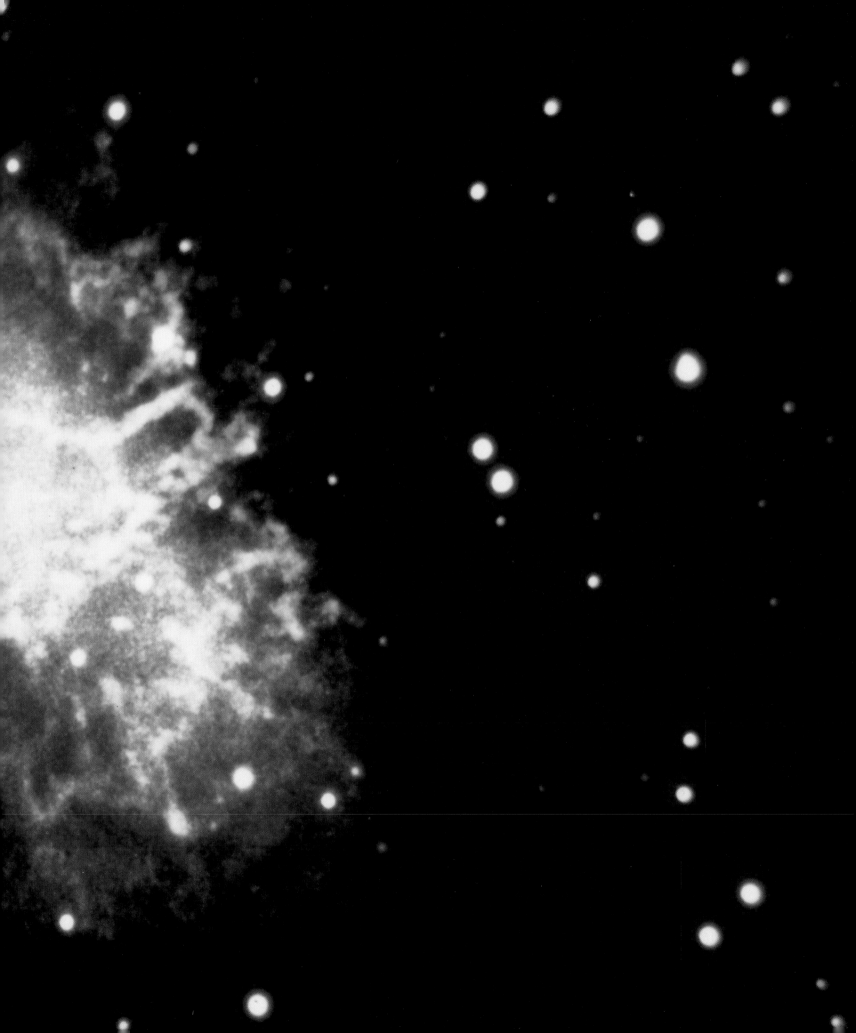

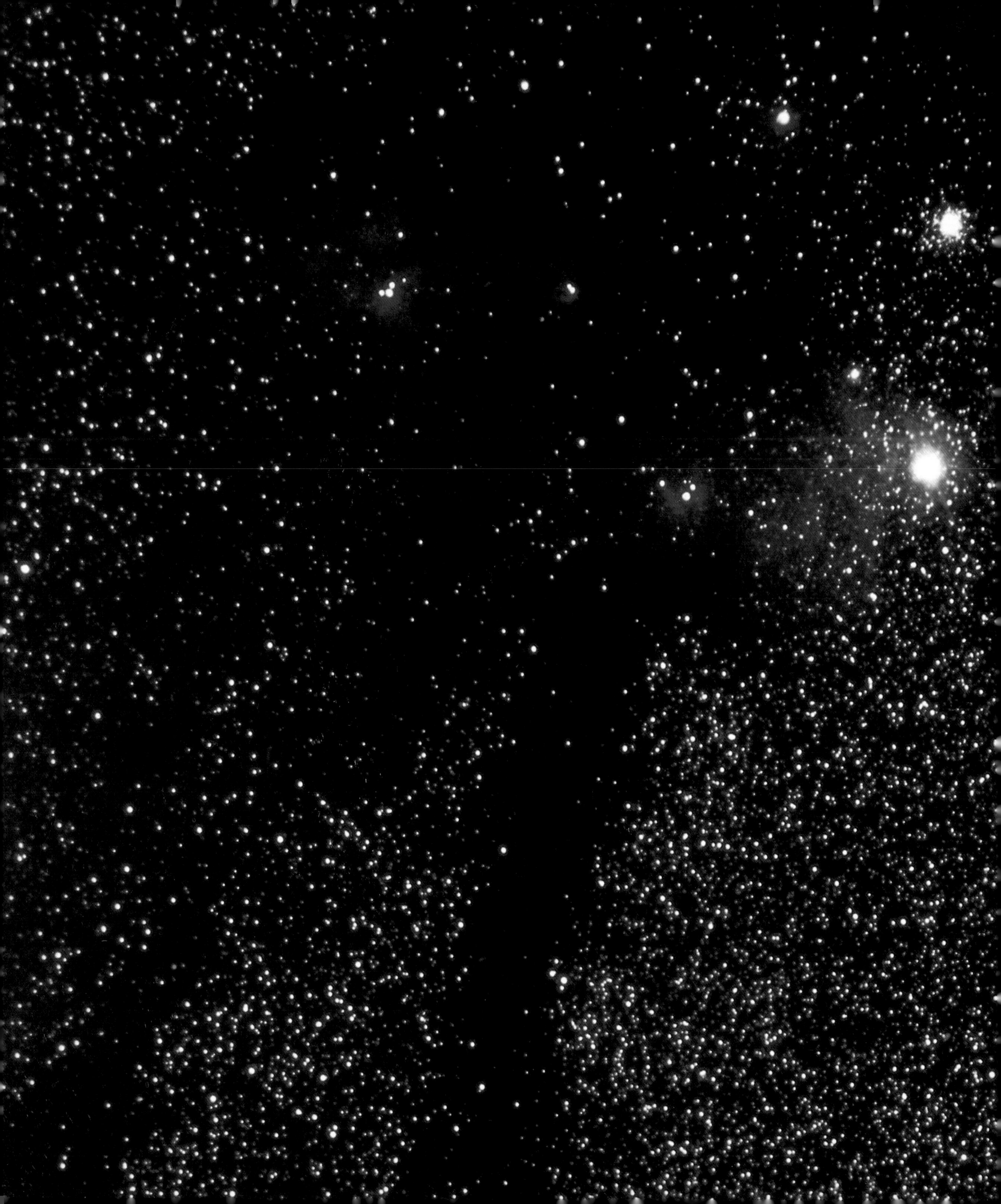

The closest quasar to Earth is about five billion light-years away. Light from this quasar began the long journey to Earth about five billion years ago, before the Earth had formed and even before the Sun began to shine. Other quasars are more than 10 billion light-years from Earth. Scientists think that the universe itself began "only" 15 billion years ago. Therefore, we see the quasars as they were near the beginning of time.

❧

We can be certain that quasars have changed in the billions of years it took for their light to reach the Earth. Many scientists believe that the quasars are galaxies that are just beginning to form. If we could see the quasars as they are now, they might resemble the galaxies that surround the Milky Way. In fact, intelligent creatures may inhabit a planet within a distant quasar. When they look into the night sky, they may see the Milky Way as it was first forming.

*Antares, a red supergiant star in the Scorpius constellation.*

Perhaps the Milky Way was once a quasar, radiating tremendous amounts of energy. Now it is a gigantic collection of 200 billion stars that spans thousands of light-years. Our seemingly endless *Galaxy* belongs to a group of thirty galaxies that we call the Local Group. Other clusters, located millions of light-years from Earth, contain thousands of galaxies. Beyond these distant collections of stars lie the mysterious quasars. Billions of light-years away, the quasars give us clues about the beginnings of our own galaxy and the beginning of time itself.

*A comet orbiting through space.*

Concord
South Side